MEL WILLIAMS

ROBERT PATTINSON

Inside Out

Piccadilly Press • London

Meet Robert Pattinson

Step aside Orlando Bloom, Daniel Radcliffe and Jude Law – the next big British movie star has arrived and his name is Robert Pattinson! For someone who only started taking a serious interest in acting when he was 15, Robert – or RPattz, as some of his millions of adoring fans call him – has had a meteoric rise to fame. However, from his heart-stopping portrayal of Edward Cullen in *Twilight*, it's easy to see why. Robert has the rare talent and smouldering physical presence all would-be screen idols crave, but few are lucky enough to possess. Not surprisingly with his gorgeous looks and natural charisma, in the past Robert has also been in demand as a model. But did you know that his star is on the rise as a musician too? He's been striving to keep it quiet, but he writes great songs with haunting melodies and heartfelt lyrics and he has a distinctive, unique singing style.

You might assume that, with the world at his feet, Robert is big-headed and aloof. But if you were lucky enough to get to talk to him, you'd find out the opposite is true – he's friendly and unassuming, and quick to play down his success, putting his soaring career path down purely to chance (as if!).

Want to find out all about the gorgeous guy behind the floppy hair and chiselled jaw?

ROBERT PATTINSON

ROBERT SAYS . . .

In How to Be, *Robert played Art, a would-be musician who is so dreadful that people walk out when he performs. He said: 'It's quite difficult to fake playing the guitar really badly when you know how to play it!'*

For instance, what was Robert like at school? What sort of girls does he fancy? What hopes does he have for the future? For the answers to these and many other essential questions, just read on. This book will tell you what Robert Pattinson is really like, inside and out.

Quick • ROBERT • Quiz

Q) Robert was the face of the 2007 Autumn/Winter advertising campaign for which luxury menswear label?

A) Hackett

OFFICIAL

ROBERT fact file...

Real name: Robert Thomas Pattinson

Stage name: Robert Pattinson

Model name: Robert Thomas-Pattinson

Musician name: Bobby Dupea

Nicknames: Rob, RPattz, Spunk Ransom

Birthday: 13 May 1986

Birthplace: London, England

Height: 6 foot 1 inch / 185 cm

Eyes: Blue-grey (and dreamy!)

Hair: Brownish-blond (and strokeable!)

Parents: Clare and Richard Pattinson

Siblings: Robert has two older sisters, Elizabeth and Victoria

Home: London, England

Iome sweet home

obert was born under the star sign of Taurus, so you would expect him to be very close to s family and happy at home – Taureans are said to love stability and security, to dislike ıange to their living environment, and to be devoted to their parents and siblings.

Robert's parents have been described as 'arty'. When Robert was young, his mother, lare, didn't have an ordinary job in an office or shop, but worked for an agency in the amorous world of modelling. Robert has joked that his father, Richard, was a second-hand r dealer, but in fact his ork was much cooler and ore stylish than that – he n a business importing ntage cars from America.

Robert was the baby of e family – and the only oy. His sister Elizabeth is ree years older and his ter Victoria is five years s senior. Robert didn't em to mind being ıtnumbered by older omen, however. In fact, let his sisters enjoy aying at dressing him ı as a girl and calling m Claudia – until he ıs 12 years old!

Robert's roots

Robert grew up in a part of London called Barnes, which is quite like a quaint village, with characterful old houses and buildings, including a popular arts centre called The Old Sorting Office, which is a venue for theatre performances. Famous rock and pop stars often hang out in Barnes because there is a renowned recording studio on Church Road, called Olympic Studios.

Quick • ROBERT • Quiz

Q) When Robert was a child, how much pocket money did his parents give him?

A) Robert earned his own pocket money; He started doing a paper round when he was about 10, earning £10 per week. He says he was obsessed with earning money until he was about 15.

FAST FACT!

According to Chinese astrology, Robert was born in the Year of the Tiger. Tiger people are charming, with magnetic appeal, who are great fun to be around. However, they can sometimes also be sensitive, moody, and like to spend time on their own. Sound like Robert?

A musical youth

Music was, in fact, Robert's first love. He started playing the piano when he was about three years old – his feet must have been dangling from the piano stool and his nose hovering just above the keys! Little Robert enjoyed learning how to play so much that he wasn't content with just one instrument. When he was only five, he also began to learn the guitar. He soon became good at performing classical guitar pieces.

Robert was so keen on music and showed such promise that if anyone had predicted what he might grow up to become, they would have been highly likely to say 'a musician'. His parents must have encouraged all of their children to pursue an interest in music, since Robert's sister Lizzy has in fact gone on to become a professional singer-songwriter.

Robert's childhood passion for music has also lasted his whole life.

COULD DO BETTER!

Robert's first school was a private all-boys school called Tower House, in East Sheen, not far from his home. Like most schools, it had a drama club and Robert took part from the age of six. He acted in several productions, such as being the King of Hearts in *Spell for a Rhyme,* a play written by one of his teachers, and playing a minor character, Robert, in an adaptation of William Golding's famous novel, *Lord of the Flies.* However, he never stood out as being a great actor. Robert just enjoyed taking part in these school productions as many of his friends did.

In fact, Robert didn't really shine at school at all. If anyone had told the teachers there he would one day play the role of ideal pupil Cedric Diggory, prefect at Hogwarts, they would probably have laughed out loud. Caroline Booth, the school secretary of Tower House, has described Robert as being 'not particularly academic', which means he never got very good grades. In a 1998 newsletter, he was also said to be 'a runaway winner of last term's Form Three untidy desk award'! Robert was sometimes naughty too. For instance, he remembers being a lunch monitor and nicking people's chips!

And here's a mystery for you. At the age of 12, Robert was expelled from Tower House *but no one knows why.* Thousands of his fans worldwide have nearly been driven crazy with wondering and trying to find out. All Robert has said on the matter is: 'I was quite bad.' So if you ever get the chance to meet him, see if you can persuade him to tell you!

Must try harder

After leaving Tower House, Robert went to another private school, the Harrodian School in Barnes, which was for both boys and girls. You might think that Robert would have tried to turn over a new leaf – however, he still didn't put much effort into his studies. He never bunked off lessons because he liked his teachers, but he hardly ever bothered to do his homework. As you can imagine, Robert's school reports were always pretty bad. His parents must have been frustrated, as they were paying expensive school fees for Robert to be a pupil there.

Robert the rapper

Robert may not have shown much interest in schoolwork, but he was still passionate about music. Although he dropped learning classical guitar at the age of about 12, he kept up his piano-playing all through his teenage years. Like most young people, Robert got really into chart music – rap in particular. He became a big fan of rap superstar Eminem and Jay Kay, the lead singer of funk band Jamiroquai.

Spreading his wings

It must have been clear to Clare and Richard Pattinson from seeing Robert's flair for music that, although their teenage son didn't seem to be suited to do well academically, he would excel if he had opportunities to develop the creative side of his personality.

FAST FACT!

At school, someone once stole the laces out of Robert's shoes. Robert continued to wear the shoes without laces for years afterwards – he felt as though they became his personal trademark!

ROBERT SAYS . . .

Robert liked his English teacher, because she encouraged him to think and write instead of just giving a basic answer to a question. Robert has said: 'I used to hand in 20 pages of nonsense and she'd still mark it. She was a really amazing teacher.'

As Clare Pattinson worked for a modelling agency, she would have known that her son's good looks and personality would be ideal in front of a camera. It was a natural step to get Robert involved in modelling and he did several photographic jobs from age 12 ('When I stopped looking like a girl,' as Robert says) to age 15.

When Robert was 13, he watched the film *One Flew Over the Cuckoo's Nest* and was captivated by the lead actor, mega-star Jack Nicholson. Robert has since said: 'I used to try and be him in virtually everything I did, I don't know why . . . I dressed like him. I tried to do his accent. I did everything like him.'

THE BARNES THEATRE COMPANY

presents:

★ GUYS AND DOLLS
★ OUR TOWN
★ ANYTHING GOES
★ MACBETH
★ TESS OF THE D'URBERVILLES

Into the spotlight

Robert has said, 'My dad wanted me to be an actor', and that Richard had some 'weird foresight' that that was what his teenage son should be doing.

One evening when Robert was 15, he was out for dinner with his dad at the Tootsie's hamburger joint in Barnes when they fell into conversation with a group of pretty girls at a nearby table. Richard asked them where they had been, and they replied that they were friends from a local drama group, the Barnes Theatre Company, which was based just around the corner from the Pattinsons' house.

Straight afterwards, Richard said, 'Son, that is where you need to go.' He kept nagging Robert on and on about it for so long that Robert eventually gave in and joined up. He didn't agree to take part in the acting, but just said he'd be part of the backstage crew – and he was only finally persuaded because he knew he'd be surrounded by attractive would-be actresses like the girls he'd met in Tootsie's.

ROBERT SAYS . . .

Once when Robert was asked by an interviewer what his motivation was for starting acting, he said it was 'a social thing. I literally went there one hundred per cent to meet these girls sitting at the next table.'

Addicted to acting!

The Barnes Theatre Company was run by experienced actors who put on two shows a year, produced to a very high standard. Everyone involved was so enthusiastic that, after working behind the scenes on one play, Robert thought perhaps he'd take his dad's advice after all and give acting a go. The next show was to be the musical *Guys and Dolls*, and, when the auditions came around, Robert put himself forward to be in front of the scenery this time, not behind it. He even wanted to play the lead – the character of Nathan Detroit, who in the movie version of the show was played by the legendary singer and actor, Frank Sinatra. So did Robert win the starring role? No, he was given a very small background part as a Cuban dancer. But Robert wasn't put off. He took on the role and performed it the best he could – even though he found it somewhat embarrassing!

The next show was a three-act play by Thornton Wilder called *Our Town,* which follows the everyday lives of citizens in small-town America in the early twentieth century – particularly the life of doctor's son, George Gibbs. And this time, Robert *did* win a lead role – the character of George himself. He gave a brilliant performance and from then on there was no holding him back. Robert appeared in several other amateur productions, such as the musical *Anything Goes* (as Lord Evelyn Pakleigh), the Shakespeare play *Macbeth* (as Malcolm, the King of Scotland), and a play adaptation of Thomas Hardy's classic novel, *Tess of the D'Urbervilles* – in which he played a lead role, the villainous character of Alec Stoke-d'Urberville. Robert's acting was so outstanding that a theatrical agent who was on the look-out for new talent approached him and signed him up!

Robert's career takes off

It wasn't long before Robert's agent had found him auditions for several professional acting jobs. First, Robert won the supporting role of Giselher in a film to be made for TV called *The Ring of the Nibelungs*. You can imagine how thrilled 17-year-old Robert was about the opportunity – not only because he would appear on screen rather than on stage, but also because the movie was going to be shot in South Africa, plus he was going to get paid for acting for the very first time! However, as it turned out, he didn't spend his money on anything luxurious . . .

When Robert excitedly told his parents he had landed the part, his dad suggested that he should leave school, since, on top of not working very hard, he was now going to be taking four months off schoolwork for filming. However, Robert was insistent that he wanted to stay on and take his A-level exams. So his dad said that Robert could use his earnings to pay his own school fees, and he would pay him back if his exam results were good enough!

FAST FACT!

Goblet of Fire director Mike Newell said: 'Robert Pattinson was born to play the role [of Cedric] . . . he is quintessentially English with chiselled public-schoolboy good looks.'

A life-changing audition

2003

2003 proved to be an extremely big year for Robert.

The day before he had to fly out to film *The Ring of the Nibelungs*, Robert went to a meeting that had been arranged for him with Mike Newell, who was to be the director of the fourth Harry Potter movie, *Harry Potter and the Goblet of Fire*. Robert tried out for the part of Cedric Diggory. Can you believe, he didn't know much about the Harry Potter books and hadn't seen any of the previous movies? He skim-read *Harry Potter and the Goblet of Fire* just the day before the audition. But Robert went into the meeting in a brilliant mood because he was so looking forward to travelling to South Africa and getting stuck into filming *The Ring of the Nibelungs.* Robert has said about the audition for the part of Cedric: 'I went in with this complete confidence – I was convinced I had it.'

As is usual with auditions, Robert didn't hear there and then if he had got the part. He put the meeting with Mike Newell to the back of his mind and threw himself into the experience of his first film acting job. But, on the very day he arrived back in London, he had to go for a call-back audition – and was told he had won the part of Cedric Diggory!

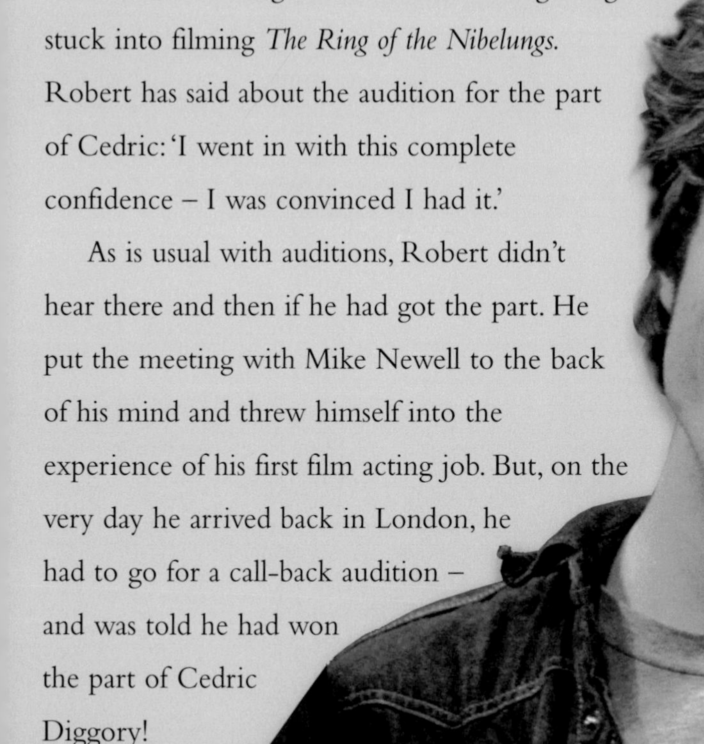

MOVIE-STAR GLAMOUR?

After the blockbusting success of the first three Harry Potter movies, not to mention the phenomenon of the series of books themselves, both Robert and his agent knew that appearing as Cedric would bring the young actor to the attention of an enormous audience worldwide. However, Robert didn't have time to think about how his life might soon change.

He had just two weeks before he had to sit his A-levels . . . and his results were – an A and two Bs! Robert has said: 'I don't know how that happened. I didn't even know half the syllabus. I'd lost faith in the exam system at that point.'

Next Robert went straight on to shoot a small part in the film version of the classic novel *Vanity Fair*, starring one of Hollywood's leading actresses, Reese Witherspoon. However, he learned the hard way that just because you take part in filming, it doesn't mean for definite that you will see yourself on the big screen. For the main, cinema version of *Vanity Fair*, all Robert's scenes ended up on the cutting-room floor! You can still see him a few times in the DVD version of the movie, though, if you pay close attention.

Quick • ROBERT • Quiz

Q) What role did Robert play in the movie *Vanity Fair*?

A) The older version of character Rawd Crawley, son of the lead character, Becky Sharp.

Hello Hogwarts

The filming of *Harry Potter and the Goblet of Fire* was movie-making on a scale Robert could never have dreamed of. In fact, few actors ever get the chance to be involved in such a humungous blockbuster in their entire career. Here's why:

The book – the fourth in the series – had been subject to even more hype than the others, because one of the main characters actually dies in the story. (The character was of course Cedric Diggory, to be played by Robert.) The filming of the movie was going to take an entire year. The sets were enormous and elaborate – including an 18-metre-deep pool and a maze with hydraulically-operated hedges. Shooting many of the scenes required around 2,000 people on set!

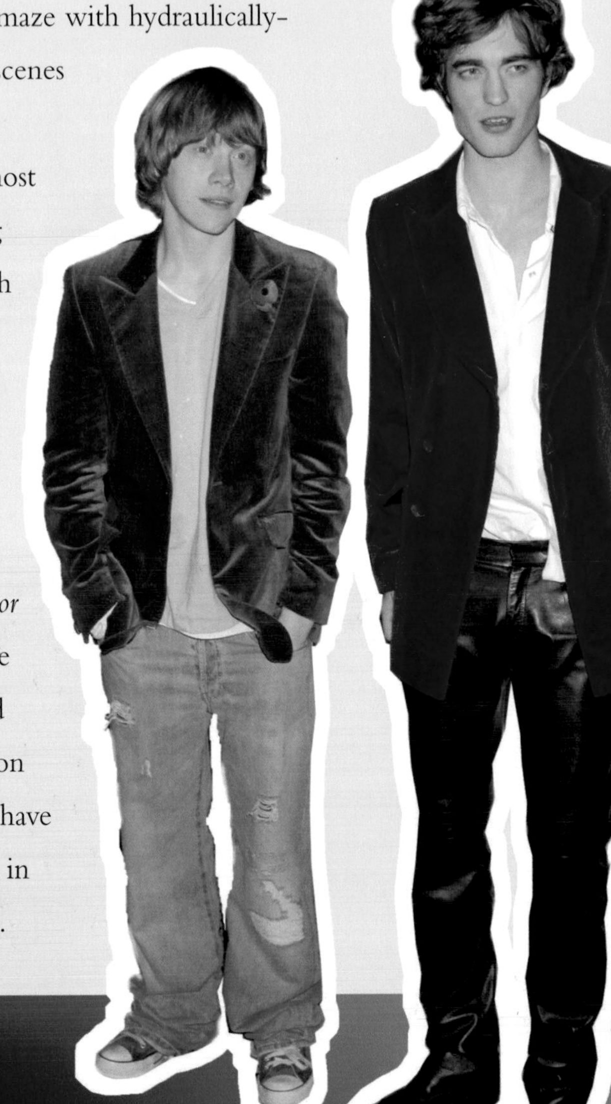

The film was to feature some of the most distinguished names in the British acting industry, such as: Oscar-nominated Ralph Fiennes and Maggie Smith, Alan Rickman (the Sheriff of Nottingham in Kevin Costner's *Robin Hood: Prince of Thieves*, Gary Oldman (whom you may know from the *Batman* movies), David Tennant (TV's *Doctor Who*); Robbie Coltrane (star of *Cracker*), and Miranda Richardson (whom you may have seen as Queenie in TV's *Blackadder*).

It's no wonder that to begin with, Robert felt daunted and apprehensive – like many of the young actors involved. To help the Hogwarts' pupils relax and bond with each other, a week was arranged before filming began when they did lots of improvisation, as a way of getting to know each other and getting into their characters. Robert often paired up with Rupert Grint, who plays the character of Ron Weasley.

Fortunately for Robert, when shooting began, the first scene he had to film – the challenge in the maze – involved only Daniel Radcliffe (Harry Potter), the producer and a crew of about 150 people. It was good to have this less overwhelming start to filming before he was plunged into the maelstrom of activity on the massive sets of later scenes. Then, inexperienced Robert tried to be super-smooth as a way of coping with his nerves. He has said: 'I was a real prat for the first month. I didn't talk to anyone. I just drank coffee and told everyone I was 24 and this famous theatre actor just back from South Africa.' But soon 18-year-old Robert settled into the experience and relaxed back into being his usual likeable self.

FAST FACT!

The scene Robert was most looking forward to filming was the cemetery scene in which he gets murdered. Asked why, he said: 'You don't really get to die that often, you know?'

What did Robert think about his young co-stars in *Harry Potter and the Goblet of Fire*?

Robert has said that it was weird being around the three main stars of the Harry Potter films, because they were so famous that they were well on their way to becoming icons! But as he worked with them closely for nearly a year, he made really good friends with his co-stars.

Daniel Radcliffe (Harry Potter): Daniel is three years younger than Robert but Robert thought that he was already an acting pro. He has said: 'He's so far superior to me in terms of desirability . . . I think Dan could steal anybody's girlfriend!'

Rupert Grint (Ron Weasley): Robert is two years older than Rupert, with whom he got on particularly well. Robert has said: 'He's incredibly funny as a real person.' Robert thinks that Rupert is a really versatile actor.

Emma Watson (Hermione Grainger): Emma first said she wanted to be an actress at the age of six, but she had only acted in school plays before the Harry Potter movies. Robert has said: 'She's an incredibly intelligent young person.'

> ROBERT SAYS . . .
> *'I think [Cedric's] a pretty cool character. He's not really a complete cliché of the good kid in school. He's just quiet. He is actually just a genuinely good person, but he doesn't make a big deal about it or anything.'*

Stanislav Ivanevski (Viktor Krum): Bulgarian-born Stanislav was spotted by a Harry Potter casting director while attending an International School in London. Robert has said: 'I started on the same day as Stan. Stan and I did a lot of on-screen stuff together, so we bonded well.'

Katie Leung (Cho Chang): Katie queued for four hours to get her two-minute audition for the part of Cho. Robert said he got on really well with Katie, commenting: 'She's a really cool girl.'

Clémence Poésy (Fleur Delacour): Clémence's father is an actor, theatre director and playwright who gave her her first professional acting job when she was 14. She had a number of film, TV and stage roles before *Goblet of Fire*. Robert and Clémence became firm friends.

Shaping up

An interviewer once enquired what similarities Robert thought he shared with his character, Cedric. He replied: 'I am generally quite pleasant – I think he is too . . . and I am relatively sporty.' However, at the start of filming, people didn't think Robert was sporty enough! Cedric is meant to be the sports star at Hogwarts and so, of course, Robert had to look super-fit – he even had to appear in a pair of swimming trunks! Robert can remember, when he was trying on the swimming trunks, the costume designer said, 'Aren't you supposed to be fit? You could be playing a sissy poet or something!' Straight away, he was given a personal trainer – one of the Harry Potter stunt team, who Robert has described as 'the most absurdly fit guys in the world'. The stunt man drew up a rigorous programme of workouts which Robert found extremely tough going – at the time, he couldn't even do ten press-ups!

On top of his punishing exercise schedule, Robert and the other Triwizard Tournament entrants had to have diving training. He remembers: 'We had to do this scene looking like heroes diving into the lake. They had a stand-in doing perfect dives on the first take. Then Stan, Clémence and I tried, but none of us could dive in right, and we all looked really stupid.' Robert had to do scuba lessons for the underwater filming too. He learned in a small practice tank and found it fairly easy. But he has said: 'I didn't see the big tank until they first started shooting in it. It was about a hundred times bigger than the practice tank and it was so much deeper, so that was sort of scary . . .'

In fact, most of Robert's scenes were action scenes, whether it was fighting off the attacking branches in the maze, battling a dragon or clashing with evil wizards. The eleven months of filming were draining, yet exhilarating.

Life after Cedric

When Robert finished filming *Goblet of Fire*, he was exhausted. As with all films on this scale, there would be months of post-production work before the movie was released and Robert would become known across the world as the Hogwarts hero, Cedric. In the meantime, Robert said his instinct was 'just to sort of collapse'. The next sort of work he wanted was definitely a short project – either a very small-scale film or perhaps a short run in a theatre play, for a complete change. In May 2005, Robert landed a part in a West End play at the Royal Court Theatre called *The Woman Before*. However, rehearsals did not go well – maybe he was just too worn out after the acting marathon that was *Goblet of Fire*? He was fired shortly before opening night! Reflecting on the experience, Robert explained: 'The acting's come along by accident. I've never trained or anything . . . On Harry Potter I was so conscious of the fact that I didn't know what I was doing, I used to sit on the side of the set throwing up. I think I will go to drama school . . . I need to learn some of the fundamentals – like how to act!'

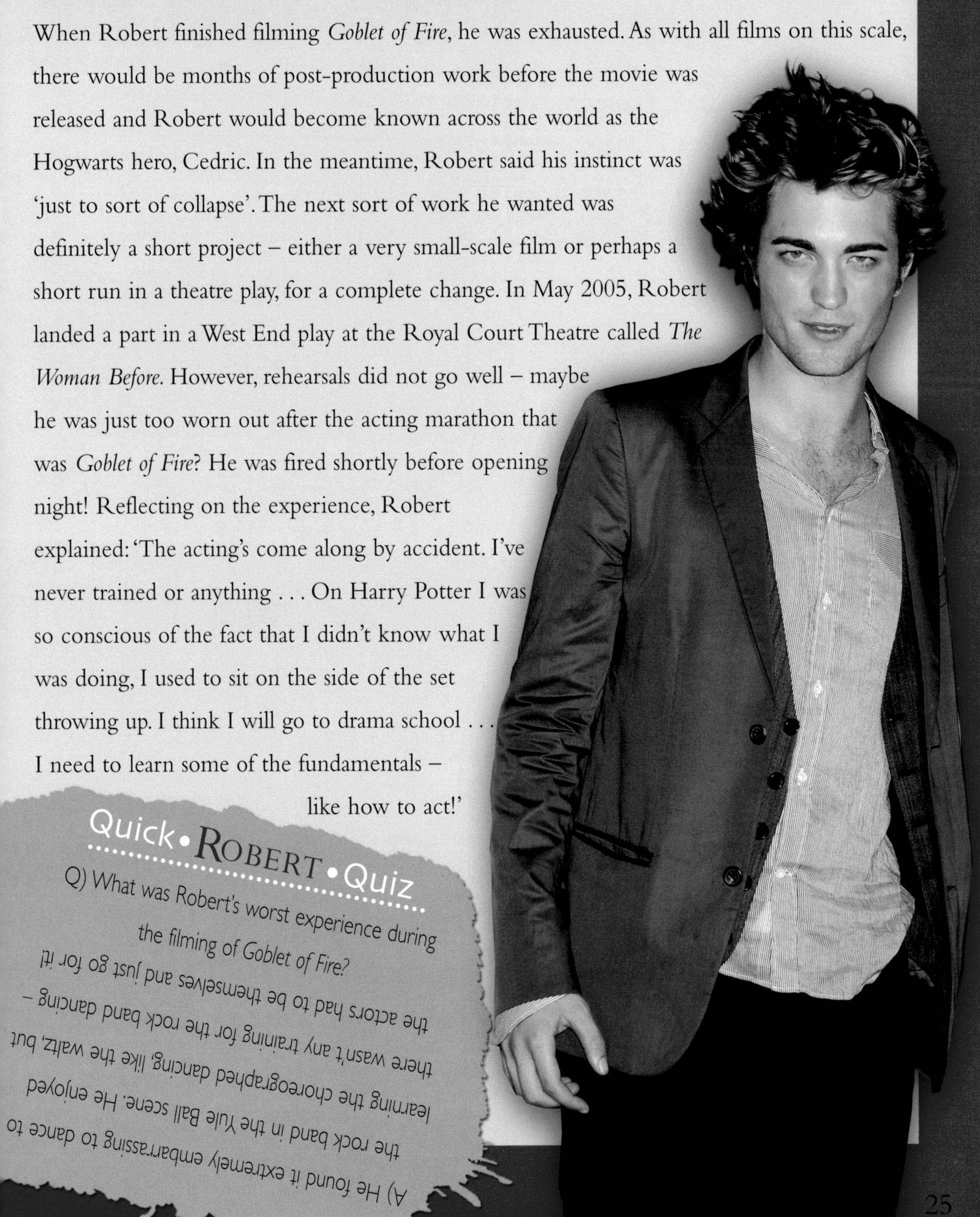

Quick • Robert • Quiz

Q) What was Robert's worst experience during the filming of *Goblet of Fire*?

A) He found it extremely embarrassing to dance to the rock band in the Yule Ball scene. He enjoyed learning the choreographed dancing, like the waltz, but there wasn't any training for the rock band dancing – the actors had to be themselves and just go for it!

2005

An overnight sensation

Of course, hanging over Robert was the knowledge that the three previous Harry Potter films had been massive blockbusting successes and the whole world was eagerly waiting for the *Goblet of Fire* as the next instalment. Robert was immensely nervous about what the fans and critics would think of his performance. For months before the world premiere in November he had nightmares about the star-studded event – huge showbiz names like Madonna had been invited to watch! Robert has said he was so jittery, he couldn't decide what to wear. So he went to Jasper Conran and picked out 'the most ridiculous, extravagant clothes – they looked really good in the shop. And then I put them on and I thought: You look such an idiot!'

On the night of Sunday 6 November 2005, Robert walked up the red carpet to the Leicester Square Odeon in front of around 12,000 clamouring Harry Potter fans and a barrage of the world's press. Many of the media and fans had camped out all night in the winter cold to ensure they got good vantage points! Afterwards, Robert said: 'I was in a trance the whole way through it. The day before, I was just sitting in Leicester Square, happily being ignored by everyone. Then suddenly strangers are screaming your name. Amazing!'

The opening of *Harry Potter and the Goblet of Fire* turned out to be the most successful movie opening ever in the UK – the film took £14.9 million in its first weekend. That year, it earned over $896 million worldwide, making it the highest grossing film of 2005. The DVD became the fastest selling DVD of all time. And while fans worldwide flocked in their millions to see it, the critics applauded the film too – particularly the way the young leads portrayed the emerging maturity of their teenage characters, putting across subtle emotions and dealing with the dark overall tone.

Suddenly, every entertainment show and magazine worldwide wanted interviews and photographs of the *Goblet of Fire* stars – and all at once, everyone seemed to know Robert's name and instantly recognise his face. He could no longer go out without paparazzi tracking him down and members of the public stopping him in the street and asking for his autograph.

Swamped by attention, Robert's life was totally transformed. He said at the time: 'It is unbelievable that this stroke of luck has completely changed my entire life. I can't even remember what I was thinking two years ago.' Whichever way would his career take him next?

ROBERT SAYS . . .

'Harry Potter is what made me become an actor. I credit Harry Potter with everything else that's come since for me.'

A CAREER CROSSROADS

After his screen-stealing performance as Cedric Diggory in *Harry Potter and the Goblet of Fire*, Robert found himself widely acclaimed in the British press as 'the next Jude Law'. As someone who had never had any serious drama training, the pressure on him to find outstanding productions in which he could turn out amazing performances must have been immense. Marked out as a hot young talent, Robert signed with an American agent in LA, and found himself being flown out to all sorts of meetings with Hollywood movie producers to discuss upcoming possible projects.

However, Robert wasn't at all sure what it would be best for him to do to develop his acting ability. He was offered some big contracts – but they seemed too overwhelming. For instance, he was once asked to sign up for three films in one go, a huge commitment which the uncertain young actor wasn't comfortable with. And in some cases, the scripts Robert felt were right for him didn't come his way – for instance, in auditions for one part Robert really wanted, he got down to the last two . . . and then the casting people picked the other actor!

FAST FACT!

You can see Robert reprise his role as Cedric Diggory in the fifth Harry Potter movie: Harry *Potter and the Order of the Phoenix*, which opened in 2007. But this is actually a 'flashback' scene from *Goblet of Fire*.

ROBERT SAYS . . .

Robert doesn't moan about the long hours and intense effort involved in filming, and he doesn't let the cut-throat aspect of auditions and ruthless side of showbusiness get him down. He has said: 'Sometimes I think, "To hell with acting," and then I realise I could be working at a shoe shop. Acting is much cooler.'

One thing Robert did know for definite was that after Harry Potter he wanted to test himself by doing 'something weird', as he once put it. And he was prepared to wait for the right role to come along. As he said at the time: 'I don't really know what I should be doing yet, so I prefer to do nothing really!'

A WALK ON THE DARK SIDE

2006

The perfect opportunity Robert was waiting for turned out to be a TV film called *The Haunted Airman,* which appeared on the BBC in 2006. Based on a 1948 novel by Dennis Wheatley called *The Haunting of Toby Jugg*, the film tells the story of a wounded, traumatised World War Two RAF pilot (Toby Jugg – played by Robert) who is sent to a convalescence home in Wales, under the watchful eyes of his aunt and his psychiatrist. Toby suffers from guilt and paranoia that manifest as terrors and visions – or perhaps he's actually imprisoned in a private hell and tormented by the spirits of the dead . . .

If there was ever a part more different from the beautiful, heroic Cedric Diggory – and one which would really challenge an actor's abilities – this was it. Toby Jugg was a complex, tortured and slightly deranged character, and Robert gave a brilliant performance, even though he was confined to a wheelchair all the way through. A reviewer in *The Stage* said: 'Pattinson – an actor whose jawline is so finely chiselled it could split granite – played the airman of the title with a perfect combination of youthful terror and world-weary cynicism.' Surely now Robert began to feel that his acting capabilities were living up to his fame.

Is he bovvered?

2007

After fighting dragons in *Goblet of Fire* and demons in *The Haunted Airman,* Robert next turned his hand to something much more light-hearted and bang up-to-date. This was a modern comedy-drama TV series which aired in 2007 – an adaptation of a novel by Kate Long called *The Bad Mother's Handbook*. The story followed a year in the lives of three different types of mother: a thirty-something woman called Karen, her mother, Nan, and her 17-year-old daughter Charlie, all trying to live together in the same, very small house, all with their own problems and secrets.

Robert played the part of Daniel Gale, a socially awkward young man who develops a crush on Charlie – even though she has just been dumped by her boyfriend and discovered that she's pregnant. It was huge fun for him to act alongside talented comedienne and actress Catherine Tate (who played Karen) – who had had huge success with her sketch programme, *The Catherine Tate Show*. Working with BAFTA nominated artists such as Catherine Tate, Anne Reid (who played Nan) and director Robin Sheppard taught Robert yet more new, crucial lessons about the skills involved in different types of acting. You could say that instead of having gone to drama school for training, Robert had set out to learn on the job.

The BIG SCREEN beckons once again

By now, Robert must have felt he was ready in both his personal and professional life to take on another blockbuster Hollywood movie. He won an irresistible role – that of a vampire who is 108 years old yet appears to be only 17, and who has the ability to read minds, along with superhuman speed and strength! This is of course the part of Edward Cullen in the movie *Twilight.*

The film is based on the 2005 novel of the same name by Stephenie Meyer – a book which was translated into 20 languages, became a *New York Times* bestseller, and won awards such as *Publishers' Weekly* Best Book of the Year, Amazon.com Best Book of the Decade So Far, and an American Library Association Top Ten Best Book for Young Adults accolade.

The plot of *Twilight* has been described as a Gothic Romeo-and-Juliet-type love story. Seventeen-year-old Isabella Swan moves to the small town of Forks, Washington, to live with her father. She is captivated by a mysterious classmate, Edward Cullen, and they fall deeply in love – despite the fact that Edward is a vampire. But Bella's life becomes endangered when three nomadic vampires arrive in town. Can Edward and his family save her – and themselves?

Quick • Robert • Quiz

Q) Does Robert like watching horror movies?

A) He has said: 'I don't like that "hiding behind doors" element when suddenly it's like: "Boo!" I like the more eerie and disturbing horror flicks. One of my favourites is *The Exorcist*.'

ROBERT SAYS . . .

'The thing I found interesting (about Edward) is that he is essentially the hero of the story but violently denies he is the hero.'

Living up to expectations

The novel was the first in a series and Robert was aware before he even started filming the movie adaptation that the books had an enormous fan-base worldwide – which was still growing at a pace. As a result, the film – released at the end of 2008 – drew a huge following from the moment the cast was announced.

Robert must have been horrified to find that postings were instantly appearing all over the internet from fans of the book who weren't at all happy that he had been cast as their hero, Edward. There was even an online petition to protest! Some readers moaned that Robert didn't have the right looks to portray Edward the way Stephenie Meyer had described him. Other readers complained that having seen Robert die as the wholesome Cedric Diggory, they would never be convinced by him as

an all-powerful, mysterious vampire. However, as soon as trailers and scene-snippets from the movie were screened, fan opinion did a drastic about-turn. Suddenly 'Twilighters' across the globe couldn't get enough of Robert as Edward – there was an online petition with thousands of signatures in support of him playing the role, and instead of hate mail, Robert was being emailed marriage proposals! The director of the movie, Catherine Hardwicke, said: 'I feel like a genius to have chosen him for the part.'

FAST FACT!

Robert's *Twilight* co-star, Kristen Stewart (Bella Swan) is four years younger than him. Her father is a TV producer and her mother is a scriptwriter. She has acted since childhood, playing alongside superstars such as Jodie Foster, Sharon Stone and Dennis Quaid. Robert has said: 'Kristen is the best actress of our generation.'

Quick • ROBERT • Quiz

Q) Who is Robert's favourite ever vampire?

A) He likes the original Nosferatu, Max Schreck.

Robert gets intimate

Making *Twilight* was a totally different experience for Robert from filming *Harry Potter and the Goblet of Fire*.

For the very first time, Robert had to put on an American accent for the part. Robert even spoke in his American accent between takes, so he didn't run the risk of slipping in and out of it during filming.

Besides the fact that Cedric Diggory is a supporting part and Edward Cullen is a lead role, the personalities of the two characters are very different. Also, Robert's scenes as Cedric Diggory were largely action-orientated, whereas being Edward was often intense, up-close and personal. Robert has said that *Twilight* is 'just about a love story rather than a massive adventure and an entire world', like *Goblet of Fire*.

Robert had to get used to doing lots of snogging in front of his co-stars and film crew, as the key relationship scenes required Rob to kiss Kristen Stewart (lucky girl!).

The 'Daniel Radcliffe' of *Twilight*?

In July 2008, five months before the movie was due to premiere, Robert and some of his co-stars appeared at a huge convention for superhero, fantasy and sci-fi fans called Comic-Con in San Diego. Robert was highly nervous, as 6,500 die-hard *Twilight* fans had travelled there to meet the actors in person and participate in a panel discussion and autograph-signing session – the queue to get into the *Twilight* area of the convention stretched for three-quarters of a mile around the building! However, as it turned out, Robert had nothing to worry about.

He took the stage to shrieks of "We love you!" and questions like, "Boxers, briefs or nothing?"

Judging by the reaction of the fans at Comic-Con, *Twilight* was set to be a movie phenomenon that would rocket Robert into acting mega-stardom. When asked what it was like to be the star of such an anticipated film, Robert answered: 'It's kind of terrifying in a lot of ways. I still can't come to terms with it.'

Adding to the pre-premiere pressure, the director of *Twilight*, Catherine Hardwicke, predicted even greater things to come from Robert, suggesting he could be the new Johnny Depp. 'His career could be extremely unique,' she said. 'He's a powerful, sexy leading man and slips incredibly well into different periods and styles. I'd love to see him work on Tim Burton-esque films where he has the opportunity to create completely wild, original characters that become classics.'

Robert must have been biting his nails with nerves. Would his performance as Edward Cullen live up to everyone's expectations?

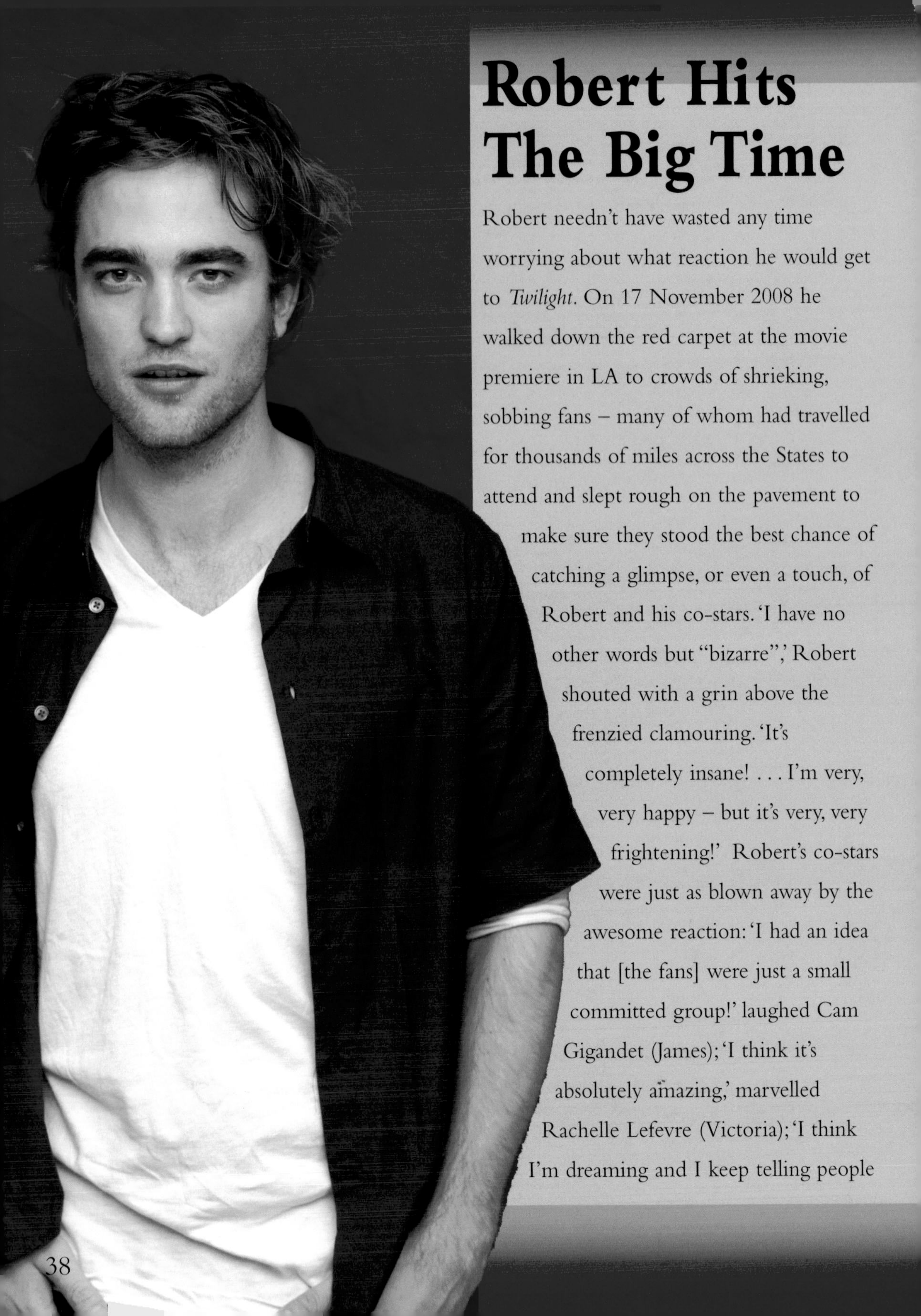

Robert Hits The Big Time

Robert needn't have wasted any time worrying about what reaction he would get to *Twilight*. On 17 November 2008 he walked down the red carpet at the movie premiere in LA to crowds of shrieking, sobbing fans – many of whom had travelled for thousands of miles across the States to attend and slept rough on the pavement to make sure they stood the best chance of catching a glimpse, or even a touch, of Robert and his co-stars. 'I have no other words but "bizarre",' Robert shouted with a grin above the frenzied clamouring. 'It's completely insane! . . . I'm very, very happy – but it's very, very frightening!' Robert's co-stars were just as blown away by the awesome reaction: 'I had an idea that [the fans] were just a small committed group!' laughed Cam Gigandet (James); 'I think it's absolutely amazing,' marvelled Rachelle Lefevre (Victoria); 'I think I'm dreaming and I keep telling people to pinch me,' gasped Taylor Lautner (Jacob). No one could believe it when the mass hysteria of the huge crowds at the British premiere on 3 December 2008 in London was even more crazy – the media described it as 'like Beatlemania with fangs!'. Typically modest, Robert said: 'It's absolutely mad – but they're here for the character, not for me.'

In its first weekend in US cinemas, *Twilight* outsold the new James Bond film *Quantum of Solace* and *High School Musical 3*. It even set a new record for the biggest ever opening weekend for a female-directed film, taking $70.6 million. *Twilight* rocketed to the top of the box offices in Britain and all round the world. It was clear that the film, made on a budget of only $38 million (small, by Hollywood standards), was not just a successful cult movie but a certified blockbuster.

'Twilight' film premiere, Tokyo, Japan

AN AWARD-WINNING ACTOR

With the incredible success of *Twilight* at the box office, surely it was only a matter of time before awards began to roll in for the movie and its star. However, accolades for *Twilight* wouldn't be the first honours Robert had ever won for his acting. The young actor hadn't just sat about waiting to see if the vampire-romance would make his name, he had also played the lead role in a British-made comedy film called *How to Be*, which was screened during 2008 at various movie events. Robert's outstanding performance as Art – an insecure, depressed, social misfit – had in October won him the award for Best Actor in a Feature Film at the Strasbourg International Film Festival. That same month, at the twelfth annual Hollywood Film Festival, Robert had been singled out as the most promising newcomer in the film business – he was awarded the New Hollywood Award.

The talk of the town

In February 2009, cinema's new heart-throb was asked to attend the Hollywood bash of all Hollywood bashes – the Oscars, to join young actress Amanda Seyfried on stage to present a montage of 2008 movie romance. Later, Robert rubbed shoulders with the movie world's finest at the hottest ticket in town, the *Vanity Fair* Oscar Party, held at the Sunset Tower Hotel. Invited to mix with the Hollywood glitterati, there could be absolutely no doubt – Robert had officially 'arrived'.

Twilight rocks!

Just three months later, it was Robert's turn to accept more awards. New noise-levels were set in California's Gibson Amphitheatre at the MTV Movie Awards on 31 May when Robert walked on stage not once . . . not twice . . . not three times . . . but *four* times to collect Golden Popcorn statuettes – for Breakthrough Male Performance, Best Kiss (teasing the audience by there and then almost-but-not-quite snogging Kristen Stewart – who won Best Female Performance), Best Fight (with Cam Gigandet) and finally, the most sought-after award of all for Best Movie.

Robert and *Twilight* ruled the night!

ROBERT SAYS . . .

'I don't even think anybody knew who I was last year!'

ROBERT TAKES RISKS

Twilight fans were dying to see Robert's six-pack again in his next movie – but they were in for a shock.

In May 2009, *Little Ashes* was released, in which Robert portrayed Spanish artist Salvador Dali – complete with eccentric hat, weird moustache, and a hairstyle described by a reviewer in *Metro* as 'deeply amusing . . . think a ruff-wearing Edward Scissorhands being dragged through a thatched cottage backwards'. *Little Ashes* explores some pretty heavy themes – including Dali's love affair with poet Federico Garcia Lorca. Robert knew it was a career risk to play a character who has a gay relationship. However, like the late, great Heath Ledger in *Brokeback Mountain,* Robert wasn't afraid to stretch his acting talents or challenge people's perceptions of him. Robert wasn't phased by filming same-sex love scenes either. Shooting intimate scenes is always a rather odd experience, regardless of whether you're playing a straight or gay character. In *Twilight,* Robert couldn't get carried away kissing Kristen Stewart because he had to follow all sorts of positioning instructions. 'I have a really flat head and so it's quite difficult to get a correct angle,' he explained once, laughing. About *Little Ashes*, he commented: 'Here I am, with Javier [Beltran], who plays Lorca, doing an extremely hard-core sex scene where I have a nervous breakdown afterwards, and because we're both straight, what we were doing seemed kind of ridiculous . . . And it wasn't even a closed set. There were all these Spanish electricians giggling to themselves.'

Robert as Art in 'How to Be'

FAST FACT!

Watch out for the small-budget independent flick that Robert filmed before *Twilight* took off. In *The Summer House* he stars as Richard, a young man who cheats on his girlfriend and goes off with his new love, only to be dumped in turn – whereupon he decides he'll do whatever it takes to win his girlfriend back.

The small-budget independent movie won mixed write-ups, although the majority of critics had nothing but praise for Robert's performance. One reviewer wrote: 'Who could have believed anyone could have been credible as Dali? . . . And yet this really young man does it with subtlety and depth.'

The Twilight Saga Continues

Twilight fans will be thrilled to hear we will see Robert three more times as Edward Cullen. In May 2009 – about to film the final scenes for the second movie, *New Moon*, and with filming for the third movie, *Eclipse*, due to start in the autumn – Robert announced at the Cannes Film Festival that he had committed to the fourth and final movie, *Breaking Dawn*.

FAST FACT!

To begin with, Robert had hair extensions to create the right look for Edward Cullen. It took the stylist EIGHT hours! Rob hated them so much that the next day he insisted she yank them all out again. That's when the now-famous Edward hairdo was invented.

If you haven't read the books, be prepared for the movies to become stranger and even more dangerous than the first. *New Moon* is a story of loss and despair in which Edward and his family leave Forks because he believes he is endangering Bella's life, leaving Bella to form a strong friendship with werewolf, Jacob Black. Bella begins to think she is going mad – in the book, she hears Edward as a voice in her head, however in the movie, Edward appears to her in memories, hallucinations and nightmares. Robert has said: 'I think that a lot of people will be kind of scared by this one . . . My character goes fifty times darker than it did in the first movie.' In *Eclipse*, Bella is forced to make a terrible choice between her relationships with Edward and Jacob, while *Breaking Dawn* tells the tale of the terrifying consequences of her decision. Can Bella survive in this sinister, supernatural world?

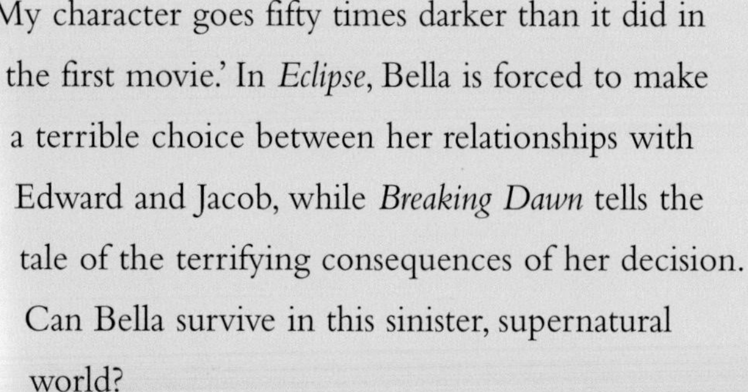

Rest assured, there will be many opportunities in the movies to admire Robert's shirtless torso once more. And he swears that his cut six-pack is all real – not given any help with the airbrush. Robert insists that his ripped abs are the result of many hours of hard slog with a personal trainer – thank goodness for us that he's prepared to suffer for his art!

Robert *at* WORK AND PLAY

In the past, Robert has said that acting came about 'by accident' and that landing his breakthrough role in *Goblet of Fire* was 'a stroke of luck' – however, this doesn't mean that he takes his career flippantly. Robert works extremely hard – he gives one hundred and ten percent effort to whichever role he is playing: he is constantly striving to improve his art by learning new acting techniques and he has had dialogue coaching for different accents and physical training for stunts. Days filming are long and exhausting – Robert may be called to a set as early as 5.30 a.m. to get into make-up and costume. Also, he often has only a couple of days off between finishing one movie and starting the next.

Down to business!

Robert also has to work incredibly hard at the business side of being an actor – and this involves giving up a lot of time to things he doesn't particularly like doing. For instance, Robert has to undertake a marathon of publicity for promoting the *Twilight* Saga. He's had to have special media training for the daily onslaught of journalists and public appearances. Robert has admitted that doing endless interviews – both face-to-face and over the phone – sometimes gets him down. He's even confessed to making up answers sometimes, to cheer himself up. For instance, he once jokingly remarked to a reporter:

'I do really intellectually highbrow stuff in my downtime. I read first-edition Shakespeare. I write poetry. I'm trying to get my Masters in neuroscience. That's the kind of guy I am . . . Man, I don't even know what a Masters is!'

However Robert doesn't mind the endless Hollywood meetings he attends to discuss new projects. 'I like meetings [in LA] a lot. You go in, no one cares if you're a nice person or not. You just do it – and if you can do it, you do it, and if you can't, you can't.' This approach appeals to Robert's no-nonsense personality.

FAST FACT!

Robert has had to have work done on his teeth, including having a brace fitted, as the Hollywood movie bigwigs reckoned his smile would be even more perfect if it was whiter and straighter!

ROBERT IN PRIVATE

Robert has never wanted to be famous and has certainly never set out to achieve mega-stardom. In a February 2008 interview he said: 'I can't see any advantage to it, because I'm happy with the life I have now.' He likes to keep his personal life low-key and private. Although he has become good pals with many of his acting co-stars, his best mates are the same two friends he has had since he was 12. He loves spending time with them because then he can just be Robert from Barnes, instead of feeling like Robert the movie star. Having time to just hang out with his family is incredibly precious to Robert too – he's so busy filming that he hardly ever gets the chance to do this any more. Robert also loves to relax by playing the piano or guitar – and he's addicted to watching *X Factor* and *American Idol* on TV too!

FAST FACT!

Robert isn't a show-off, flashy type of person and doesn't wear loads of designer labels. He has said in the past that his fashion inspiration is the 1950s actor James Dean – who was famous for his relaxed jeans-and-leather-jacket look.

Robert at home

Until 2008, Robert lived with a friend in a rented flat in Soho, London. However, he found himself spending so much time away at meetings in Hollywood, filming all over the world – from LA to Britain to Canada to Italy – and attending publicity events and premieres, that he now just lives wherever his career takes him. When Robert's settled in a hotel room, he's intensely private – he doesn't even like to let the maids in to clean! After all, it's the only place he gets any time and space to himself. There are always fans waiting outside his hotel for him – and while he's delighted to have so many followers, the phenomenal level of fame he's achieved does have its downside. He can't walk down a street any more without being swamped by admirers – and if he stopped to talk to everyone, he'd never get anywhere. He tries to disguise himself, but has said: 'I'm just getting more and more conspicuous – I'm wearing two hoods, a hat and sunglasses, which kind of stands out in the middle of the night. So I'm learning to sprint!'

Lucky in love?

Robert once modestly commented that trying to 'play beautiful' is one of the most daunting aspects of acting. He obviously doesn't realise that he doesn't have to try! He has MILLIONS of girls swooning over him – many stars among them. 'I'm a BIG fan of Robert Pattinson!' Ashley Tisdale once commented, blushing.

Robert continually has to contend with media rumours about his romantic life. He's been linked to celeb Paris Hilton, actresses Natalie Portman and Megan Fox, and *Twilight* co-star Nikki Reed; he's been reported to be dating a Brazilian model, to have stolen Camilla Belle away from one of the Jonas Brothers, and to have proposed marriage to Kristen Stewart! However, Robert told *GQ* magazine in April 2009: 'There's literally not a single [true] story that could be written about me – I never do anything.' He said he's never even met the Brazilian model, he's 'not guilty' over Camilla Belle, and the only place he's proposed to Kristen Stewart is on-set while acting. It's true that Robert once described Kristen as his 'celebrity crush' and Kristen has admitted that she thinks 'he's really hot' – but they both insist they're just good friends. Unbelievably, the sultry Robert really does seem to be single!

If you fancy your chances, just start saving! In a charity auction at the Cannes Film Festival 2009, Robert offered to sell a kiss to raise money for AIDS research. He tantalisingly commented: 'If it goes really well, maybe it'll lead to something more . . .' In the end he sold two - £17,500 for EACH smooch!

Making Music

Robert is passionate about music – he loves everything from James Brown (soul/funk) to Rachmaninoff (classical) – and not just listening, but composing and performing his own music too. However, he's been doing his best to keep his potential as a musician under wraps. In interviews, Robert always underplays the fact that he once formed a rock band called Bad Girls with some friends, and that he's written many songs and performed them at solo gigs under the pseudonym Bobby Dupea. Robert's voice is raw and his melodies are folksy and bluesy, reminiscent of the legends Bob Dylan, Emmylou Harris and Van Morrison – whom Robert has said he would love to play if a movie were ever made of the Irish singer's life.

You can hear Robert performing his songs, 'Never Think' and 'Let Me Sign' on the soundtrack of *Twilight*. When asked how they came to feature in the movie, Robert answered: 'By accident . . . Nikki [Reed] gave a CD of stuff I'd recorded on my computer to Catherine [Hardwicke]. I'd recorded it years ago . . .' Catherine herself has commented: '[Pattinson] is a great pianist – long vampire fingers! . . . His two songs are pretty great.' For now, there are no plans to put his music on *New Moon,* but Robert admits he has become obsessed with composing songs. 'I play a lot of music,' he has said. 'That's what I wanted to do before the acting thing accidentally took off – be a musician. All my best friends are musicians and they have all got their albums and deals . . .'

Surely it's only a matter of time before record bosses talk Robert into recording his own album and it goes blazing to the top of the charts.

Quick • Robert • Quiz

Q) Where did Robert get his musician's pseudonym, Bobby Dupea, from?

A) Bobby Dupea was the character Jack Nicholson (Robert's hero) played in the movie *Five Easy Pieces*, which propelled him to stardom.

The Only Way is Up!

As the hottest new young actor in Hollywood, Robert is in such demand that he is booked up for a series of projects before the filming of the *Twilight* Saga is even completed. *Remember Me* is a drama set in New York about lovers who are plagued by family tragedy. Robert will star alongside *Lost* star Emilie de Ravin and ex-007 Pierce Brosnan. For once, he plays a young man not unlike himself – no wands, fangs or funny hats required! Then, *Unbound Captives* will be a complete change – it is set in the American frontier of the mid-1800s and Robert will have to speak Comanche, a Native American language. Next Robert will travel to Paris to star in *Bel Ami*. His character is a young journalist in a corrupt society – to survive, he becomes a master seducer, blackmailer and shameless social climber. 'It's a totally amoral character,' Robert has commented, with relish.

When an interviewer once asked Robert how he selects projects, he replied: 'I like the most random scripts . . . I am really close friends with my agent – she really gets me and knows my taste . . . I barely ever like scripts, actually. I prefer to do nothing than something stupid.' In fact, one of Robert's forthcoming projects may not be a movie at all but a stage play instead. Theatre director David Pugh told *Vanity Fair* magazine that he will be working with Robert in 2010 – although he refused to say on what.

Besides acting in movies and on stage, and writing and performing music, the multi-talented Robert has many other exciting ambitions. He has started writing his own film scripts – it's been reported that one of them, based on diaries he kept as a teenager, is under consideration by an American agent. Robert has also said that in the next ten years or so he'd like to have his own film production company – and he'd like to try his hand at theatre directing too.

One thing's for certain – Robert's got the talent, the looks and the personality to be a success whichever path he chooses in future. Watch out world, here comes Mr Pattinson!

First published in Great Britain in 2009 by Piccadilly Press Ltd, 5 Castle Road, London NW1 8PR www.piccadillypress.co.uk. Designed by Simon Davis. Printed and bound in China by WKT
3 5 7 9 10 8 6 4 2

Picture credits: Getty:p3, p7, p8, p9, p10, p13, p15, p17, p18, p19, p21, p28 (left), p29 (right), p36, p47, p48, p53, p54.
Rex Features: p5, p11, p16, p20 (right), p24, p25, p27 (top), p28 (right), p29 (left), p33, p37, p38, p39, p41–45, p51, p56.
Corbis: 22/23, p26, p27 (bottom), p34/35, p49. Alamy: p2, p22 (left), p46